Contents

A Reason to Smile:

Finding Happiness in Life's Little Moments

By C.K. Murray

Similar works by C.K. Murray:

Mindfulness Explained: The Mindful Solution to Stress, Depression, and Chronic Unhappiness

Emotional Intelligence Explained: How to Master Emotional Intelligence and Unlock Your True Ability

The Confidence Cure: Your Definitive Guide to Overcoming Low Self-Esteem, Learning Self-Love and Living Happily

Health Hacks: 46 Hacks to Improve Your Mood, Boost Your Performance, and Guarantee a Longer, Healthier, More Vibrant Life

How do *you* find happiness?

No matter who you are or where you go, life will never be perfect. Some days, your world is filled with stress and sadness. Other days are neither bad nor good, yet another stretch in the haze. And for many of us, with our thoughts heavy and minds weary, hope is fading fast.

If you find yourself sinking, if you find yourself wishing there was a way to feel better, to feel happier, to stop judging, and searching, and worrying about everything you *think* you need, and want, <u>now</u> is the time to change.

Life is beautiful.

But how many times do you need to be reminded? How many times do you rest your head on the pillow at night, wishing for a different life? How many times do you close your eyes, wanting nothing more than to drift away and forget?

In today's hectic world, it's easy to get lost. Too easy. Sometimes it seems like we don't have *time* to enjoy the things around us. The little things, the small moments that remind us how good it is to be alive— just alive.

When's the last time you noticed the things that matter? Honestly, do you even know what they are?

Not your bank account, your work schedule, your errands, meetings, and all that stuff. No, no. When's the last time you took a breath, savored the air, the smell, the sights and sounds; the *experience* of living? The last time you saw the smile and curiosity on your friends' and family members' faces? Witnessed that brief but amazing glimmer of life in the people who matter most? And soaked it all in?

Truth be told, moments of happiness are all around us. They fill our days and nights, even if we barely take the time to notice. And the most important of them, the greatest, come from our most intimate source— ourselves.

But how do we unlock it? How does one go about achieving the level of power and perception that can find happiness in even life's darkest moments?

Well, the answer is *far* easier than you think…

Everyday Moments of Happiness

You don't have to be a Zen Master or <u>stress guru</u> to achieve happiness. You don't have to use illicit substances or legal prescriptions to achieve happiness. All you need to is open yourself. But before you can truly open your inner world to the light, you need to first *see* the light.

That's right, start by noticing things that are pleasing, and soon your entire perceptual framework will change. By embracing these small events and situations, you'll begin to feel more lighthearted; more content and more accepting. Allow the <u>power of mindfulness</u> to wash over you. Enjoy the moments and soak them in.

Such experiences include:

The morning glow. The way the sun pours in through an open window or is sliced by the blinds. The way that warm light caresses you to your senses. The way it slowly bleeds through your close eyelids, energizing your muscles and mind to a gentle awakening. The way it is there on weekends, when you have no worries and no plans. A guiding light; bringing you to the waking world from the realm of dreams.

Water and lather. Nothing like a nice shower, as that perfect temperature of H20 splashes, splatters, drizzles and rinses every crevice and corner of your body. It soothes your skin and relaxes your muscles.

It cleans your hair and removes your smell. Showering and bathing are incredibly relaxing, restorative, and happiness-inducing activities. Throw in some fragrant and sudsy soap, and you've got a mixture made in heaven.

Mirror magic. That feeling when you've got yourself all ready to go. Your clothes are looking right, your hair is styled, your look is hot and ready. You feel as if nothing can bring you down. You're in prime shape, looking damn good.

You feel this way for a reason. Repeated confident behaviors actually change your neurons.

Wakeful buzz. Few things beat your first cup of joe in the morning. You feel the caffeine flood your veins, the tingling in your eyes, the tasty warmth filling your mouth, throat and stomach. The way the steam hits your face.

Or maybe it's a cup of hot tea. You take a pause to savor the aroma and the taste, the gradually growing buzz as you prepare for your day.

Mind your music. Allow your favorite chords, tunes, rhythms and beats to resonate. Allow them to bring you to a special place in your heart and soul where worries and problems cannot touch you. Allow the power of music to improve your health and wellbeing. Music is a noted health hack, and you should do everything in your power to welcome its mind-altering properties.

Delicious bite. The first time you sink your teeth into that juicy burger, or crispy salad, or decadent dessert. The first savory morsel that meets your palette and tingles your taste buds. Everybody knows that the first taste, the first novel experience, is the one we remember.

Adrenaline. In case you didn't know, exercise is good for you. And the reason it's so good for you is because it sends neurochemicals flooding through you. Adrenaline and endorphins and dopamine and all sorts of mind-changing, body-powering chemicals fill us with that rush of excitement. Runners will talk of 'runner's high,' but you don't have to be an avid cardio machine to get the benefits. Simply walking at a moderate pace will get you feeling happier and easier. Of course, if you really want to maximize that high, try finishing a tough workout. The afterglow will leave you feeling incredible.

Love ping. The feeling you get when somebody you really like, love, or lust makes a connection. It can be something as simple as receiving a text; or maybe a call; or maybe kissing, snuggling, or going further with that special somebody. No matter the act, feeling that emotion will keep you coming back for more. And will leave you happier than you thought you could ever be.

Beddie bye. Nothing like seeping into your lovely mattress and locating that perfect comfy spot where your mind and body can find peace. Imagine how you feel right before you go to bed, as you shut your eyes having accomplished all you wanted in the day—having gone further than you ever imagined you would.

Nothing like drifting off to dreamland with mission accomplished.

But let's not stop there. There are plenty of changes that you take to start living happier <u>today</u>. If you really want to start feeling better about yourself and your abilities, about your shortcomings and your struggles, you need to change the way you think. Don't be somebody who collapses. Don't be somebody who gives in because they hate how they feel and believe it will never change.

Happiness is a choice.

If you want to start feeling happy, it's as easy as changing your mindset. Although this may seem like a tall task at first, it can actually become quite natural. How, you ask?

Positive Psychology: Cultivating the Power of Positive Attitude

Positive psychology has the potential to *irrevocably* change our lives for the better. It doesn't take a mentalist to make this happen. What it does take is a willingness to enjoy life and smile more often.

Sound easy enough?

Good! Then let's not waste any more time. Here are the strategies:

Step outside yourself

Sure, we all have a tendency to think of ourselves from time to time. Sometimes, our selfish behaviors might even have merit. But more often than not, they're doing us more harm than good.

If you really want to start living happier and healthier, you would be wise to remember what makes you special, and then *move on*. Don't obsess any further over treating yourself or appeasing yourself. Don't beat yourself up for perceived failures or shortcomings. Don't think that you can't be a certain way or change a certain attitude. Don't let your precious ego dictate your life.

Instead, practice humility and focus on others.

Of course, the point is a little more complicated than this. If you want to feel happy, you obviously have to think of yourself, because it's yourself that you want to change. But in thinking of yourself, think of yourself insofar as how you can improve yourself to better others. Don't do it simply to satisfy your ego.

And don't, don't tie your self-worth inextricably to external metrics. In other words, make a consistent effort to be honest with yourself. Too many people will link their self-worth to things like job performance, school performance, events with friends and family members. They'll value or devalue themselves based solely on things happening outside of themselves. While they are right to acknowledge a role in certain external events, many people become dependent on these things. Research shows that externally-focused people react to *successes* with small bursts of happiness, whereas perceived *failures*—even small ones—elicit much more powerful negative responses.

Moreover, many individuals who tie their 'failures' and 'successes' to external factors will have a higher incidence of depression, underachievement and substance abuse. This occurs because such individuals underachieve and abuse substances as a way to protect their egos. This way, if they fail, they can blame the fact that they 'didn't try' or were high or drunk. But then, if they succeed, they can attribute their success unrealistically to an incredible inner ability, an ability that they will never fully cultivate.

Abusing alcohol and drugs only serves to validate grandiose notions of ability: "Look what I did, *despite* the fact that I don't try and am messed up all the time! I don't even need to try!"

Experiences not *Things*

Everybody likes having cool things.

But the research shows that having cool things doesn't make you feel cool for long. In fact, studies show that experiences have more lasting effects than material purchases.

So-called "experiential purchases" make us happier because they have a certain living, breathing quality to them. You might like having a cool car or phone or technology, but in so many years, it's going to be outdated and unimpressive.

The reasons that experiences are so big is that they get better with time and can be relived. We can always tell stories of a fun cruise or vacation or camping trip or bachelor/bachelorette weekend. We can always tell awesome stories, and embellish them with time. Not to mention, people recall such experiences more so than they do, say, the time they bought some material possession. People are more likely to say, "Remember that crazy time at the beach?" as opposed to "remember that crazy surf board I bought at the beach?"

Experiences are unique and are shared with other individuals. They help form our character, our personal development. Material possessions do not. Our brains actually take much longer to adapt to novel experiences than they do novel materials, making experiences much more impactful. They are also impactful because they tie into our natural social need for interaction.

And social interaction, dear friends, is one of the underpinnings of vibrant longevity.

Avoid Superficiality

Once you've made the commitment to step outside of yourself, your social networks will open up. And while it's nice to have people with whom to interact and talk, you need to watch yourself. Making small talk and chatter is good for bridging the gap, but too much of the meaningless chitchat, and soon you may be finding yourself less than happy.

In fact, research indicates that *meaningful* talk—such as discussions of intimate or intellectual matters—actually increases happiness. Meanwhile, superficial conversations have a higher incidence in the lives of socially isolated and unhappy people.

Cocktail chatter is detrimental for obvious reasons. Firstly, it follows a rather boring and unstimulating etiquette that does nothing for our minds or hearts. Secondly, people who participate in small talk are likely to have fewer people with whom they truly connect—meaning they lack strong, supportive family and friends. In time, this takes its toll, as the individual suffers from an inability to express pressing matters and release the tension associated with internalized negative emotions.

This is also supported by studies that look at social networks. A lot of research linking Facebook, Twitter and Instagram 'addiction' have identified a high prevalence of depression symptoms among addicts. This is due, in large part, to the fact that such social networks become unfulfilling substitutes for real-world interactions.

Comfortably Busy

This one seems like a conundrum, until you consider the two extremes. On one hand, you have somebody who rushes to and fro, who never really takes the time to 'smell the flowers,' and who seems miserable. Then you have the sloth who never really seems to commit or accomplish anything, and may just spiral into a dark pit of depression, drugs, and self-defeat.

So what you need is balance.

All in all, studies show that productive people are more happy than people who struggle to fill their days. Of course, research cautions that being productive doesn't necessarily mean being busy. Plenty of busy people are so distracted that they never get to focus. As a result, they suffer from brain fatigue and may even experience advanced cognitive decline.

In other words, don't be afraid to turn down offers for things you don't really want to do. If you're already worn down and tired, allow time to unwind. Drink a glass or two of wine, sit in a hammock, read a book, take a bath, go for a walk or hike, go to a show, a movie, out to dinner—you name it. Don't allow work and to-dos to conquer your day.

Remember: having things to do, doesn't necessarily mean you're getting more things done. It might just mean you're cramming your hours with needless clutter. So don't clutter your mind and your life.

Find the balance that works for you! And if you have a dream, a passion, an artistic endeavor—*always* make time for it!

Quality over Quantity

This saying may not apply to money, but it sure goes far when applied to relationships. That is to say, people treasure relationships that have value. Although today's internet age seems to prize countless 'friends' and followers on social networks, research shows that the happiest people are those who have smaller, closer groups of true friends. Not to mention, having a tight-knit social network will also extend your life.

So aim for people who you can trust. Instead of trying to amass numerous acquaintances, work on connecting with much smaller numbers of confidantes. The benefits in this are obvious. By having people you can share personal info with, you have outlets. You also receive empathy, compassion, understanding, and a variety of other positive emotional forces that reduce stress and improve wellbeing.

It's also important to remember to work on your relationships. See, friendships and family relations and partnerships are living, breathing things. If you don't supply them what they need, they'll dwindle and die. So don't neglect the closest people in your life!

Stay in contact with people who matter, at least once every two weeks. Instead of social networking or texting, try to actually call them and talk! Oh, and be sure to remember important events. Celebrate their birthdays, be active and constructive during conversations, make plans and congratulate them for the good things in their lives. Also, allow them to tell you about themselves. People love to talk about themselves, so allow them to do so.

Just being more open and receptive is the key to sustaining relationships. Some people will try to reach out, but if they continue to do so without responses from you, you'll never get anywhere!

Small Moments

Research shows that small rewarding moments are in fact very powerful actors on overall happiness. In fact, consistent smaller 'rewards' are more effective than larger, periodic ones when it comes to improving happiness. The frequency is more important than the intensity.

This is why people who enjoy things like a nice dinner or dessert or sunrise or sunset on a regular basis are often more happy than people who only occasionally indulge—through things such as vacations, cruises, and other larger rewards. Of course, the trick is finding balance. If you are *always* enjoying in these indulgences, you become desensitized to their effect. Sort of like a wealthy person who can have any material thing he or she wants, but is never happy.

The best route is to reward yourself intermittently. But more than that, you have to learn to perceive rewards where before they did not exist. See your daily grind as rewarding in the sense that you are getting closer to a goal such as promotion, higher pay, more recognition, or personal achievement. Chart your relationship progress with significant others. Make incremental evaluations and reward yourself for being patient.

Just not too often!

Delayed gratification

Researchers find that self-control is paramount for happiness. People that can resist their temptations are less likely to go astray. They are less likely to engage in drug and alcohol abuse. Many psychological diagnoses, such as ADHD, are based on problems in attention, hyperactivity, and impulse control.

The trick is to use strategic distractions that keep you from doing what you compulsively want to. This allows you to get your most important things done without having to spend so much energy channeling willpower. Instead, trick yourself into thinking about other things. Hide tempting foods or beverages in locations you don't frequent. Make it a habit to take a certain route to work or home so that you avoid temptations. Don't keep certain vices in clear view or access.

Fill your head with thoughts of productive things and allow your vices to be the rewards. This will help stave off cravings. In the end, you might just find you enjoy delaying gratification… it makes gratification that much sweeter!

9.) Show Some Appreciation

Altruism, good deeds, displays of gratitude. All of these things are great ways to enhance your life and the lives of others. Something as simple as writing a thank-you note has been shown to significantly boost personal happiness.

But there are a million other simple things you can do to feel good about yourself and others. Hold the door for a stranger, leave a nice tip for a waiter, give a homeless person a fast food burger, make eye contact with a disabled person who is often shunned, go to a volunteer shelter, knock on a new neighbor's door and offer brownies—you name it.

The point is that we feel better when we make others feel better. This should be no surprise, as it likely has an evolutionary basis. We are social creatures that thrive on others. We depend on caregivers to protect us as babies until we develop our own self-protective capacities. Even then, we seek interaction. Social wellbeing is personal wellbeing.

Outlook Change

You probably don't want to hear this because it seems so broad and obvious. But consider this: research has shown that even the most basic exercises can improve happiness. Something as easy as listing a few positive things in your day can get rid of depression symptoms and boost happiness. Happiness can quite literally be taught.

Appreciating what you have is the key to happiness. It is the fundamental springboard for changing attitudes and behaviors. Instead of comparing yourself to others who you deem happier or more successful, compare yourself to yourself. In other words, look inward and see what you have done to better yourself. Understand that you don't have it nearly as bad you think you do.

But sometimes, it is good to look at others. Don't put yourself down, but be open-minded. Be welcoming to new ideas and recommendations. Motivate, don't deprecate.

And who better to model ourselves after for happiness than… happy people?

The Highly Effective Habits of Happy People

Happy people are happy because they have it figured out. But they don't have it figured out because they're smarter, or keener, or better or more successful. They have it figured out because they've made an effort to be happy. They've chosen happiness.

And that's honestly all it takes.

Get into the sun

Vitamin D has numerous health benefits, and can even treat many common ailments we like to medicate. But beyond sunshine, simply being around nature and green colors is great for us.

Merely looking at natural settings (or images) has been shown to trigger happiness, positivity, and emotional stability almost immediately. When you're out in nature, you appreciate the oft-ignored processes. Birds chirping, the smell of flowers, a nice breeze, the smell of trees, the rustle of grass, mountain ridges, beaches, and salty ocean air—these are all very important health hacks that trigger feelings of wellbeing short-term and long-term.

Get some rest!

Exemplary sleep can treat virtually all mental and physical ailments to an extent. You don't even have to get it in its traditional format. Catnaps, power naps, and a full night's sleep can all be effective. No matter the method, quality Zs will change the way you experience life, and happiness.

According to the Harvard Medical School, skimping on sleep makes us less optimistic and more likely to be depressed. It also causes to eat sugary more unhealthy foods which then exacerbate our feelings of *blehhhh.*

Mindfulness

Meditation doesn't have to come through traditional or mystical practices. You don't even have to engage in unfamiliar stretches or maneuvers. And you certainly don't have to sit completely still, humming for minutes on end.

For most of us, meditation can be equated to mindfulness, or the ability to enter the present moment. It is a very real, very advantageous practice that can be incorporated into everyday moments. So don't think that you are incapable. If you apply mindfulness several times a week for several months, you can actually change the thickness and density of your brain!

Practicing mindfulness will also allow you to detach yourself from negative feelings, thoughts, and emotions. You'll worry less about past mistakes and misadventures, and look more toward a positive future. You'll also be better able to forgive people for their mistakes—a great trait!

The Writer's Outlet

There's a reason they say journals, diaries, stories, and other written works are therapeutic.

Sometimes when we get negative thoughts and feelings in our heads, we can't get them out. They continue to circulate, feeding other nasty monsters until eventually they all collide in our hearts

This is why it's healthy to remove your thoughts through writing. By jotting down your negativity, you can see it represented before your eyes. This allows you to separate such negativity from your being. It also allows you to scrutinize such thoughts as if they are material things. Researchers indicate that throwing away recorded negative thoughts is a great way to lessen sadness. Meanwhile, recording positive thoughts and keeping them close nearby is a good way to tap back into those positive times when you're feeling down.

Toss the negative, save the positive.

Keep it sexy!

Everybody loves sex.

And now you have another reason to love it. The science of sex is incredible. Sex is not only an amazing feeling but it also increases our mood long-term, makes us happier, and has been linked to higher incomes. In some strange way, the happiness afforded by sex makes us more susceptible to money-making. Or perhaps, the correlation is less mystical—maybe rich people simply get more sex ;)

Either way, sex is great, you don't have to be some kind of guru to enjoy its benefits. Heck, you can even reap the benefits through a little 'alone time.' That said, the research finds the greatest benefits when you're with a partner. So if you have trouble *getting* a partner, up your game!

Opening the pores

Exercise will get you looking better, which will make you feel better, which will make you feel happier about how you look. But it also has instant effects when we're in the midst of it. Try going for a walk, or a run, or playing a sport, or lifting weights. Exercise releases antibodies which fight diseases and endorphins which have been linked to the famous 'runner's high.'

You can read a million studies linking exercise to health and happiness benefits. You can also read a bunch of studies indicating that exercise increases lifespan. So if you want to make something of yourself, do it! Don't be afraid to start slow. Don' feel embarrassed at the gym because you're new. Savor your ability to work hard and change your health. And if you don't have the time in your day, exercises as short as 7 minutes can have lasting effects. Simply Google "high intensity exercises" and you'll be surprised by the results.

New Pursuits

People that are happy will not pull away from intimidating or unfamiliar challenges. They will embrace new experiences and enter them with unbridled optimism. Besides, once you have conquered a new skill, you feel more knowledgeable and more capable, making you also more likely to pursue more challenges. Go for anything that interests you, whether it be writing a book, learning a language, instrument, board game, computer skills, career path, or something else.

And don't get discouraged early on. Many people will give up prematurely. Heck, you don't have to be the best at something to enjoy it! Do it because it makes you feel a certain way. Don't do it because you have to be better than somebody else.

Sometimes, our happiest moments come from doing something for no other reason than we want to.

Manage Money

There are plenty of surveys and studies showing that building a savings makes people happier. It makes you feel more secure, it allows for more experiences in life, and it generally makes things easier. However, there is also something to be said for detaching oneself from the pursuit of more money. Like anything, if you simply make money for the sake of money—your happiness can suffer. Some people have all the money in the world, but all they do night and day is think about amassing more wealth. They're so obsessed with money-making that they never get to enjoy it. Or perhaps, they're so obsessed with money-making because they have no choice—they're living lavishly and need more to continue!

Of course, the best part about making money is sharing it with others. People who share their wealth reasonably with family and friends are the most happy. This is because it is a shared experience that enhances everybody's life.

But beware. When the people capitalizing on this money *do not* genuinely appreciate it, then sharing money becomes problematic. But for the most part, it's a good experience. So go on vacation, go to a sporting event, enjoy some activities with new tools, equipment or accessories—have fun!

Self-Respect

Obviously, you need to respect yourself if you want to be happy. If you don't respect yourself, you'll feel bad. You won't deem yourself worthy of success and you'll crawl through life feeling incapable. When it comes to self-respect, self-hygiene is an important aspect.

It's easy to forget to tend to ourselves when life is so hectic, but why wouldn't we? Shouldn't our personal happiness be priority #1?

So get to it! Brush your teeth, drink plenty of water, get regular exercise, wear clothes that boost your self-esteem, groom your look, ge enough sleep, cut your fingernails, don't abuse drugs or unhealthy foods or drinks, shower regularly, and feel good about yourself!

The better you feel, the better you'll look! The better you look, the better you feel! And if need be, use a little retail therapy. Don't become attached to material things, but allow yourself the occasional indulgence. Buy new clothes, accessories, gadgets—something to make you feel less stressed and more confident in everyday life.

Don't be afraid to show off your possessions from time to time! Just don't let them define you. *You* define them.

Fuel the body

Obviously, you've heard this refrain before: Stay away from sugars, cut calories, avoid processed foods, blah, blah, blah. But when it comes to eating healthy, there is something you probably didn't know.
People who load up on a good amount of fruit and vegetables daily—7 servings—report being much happier. This is due to the nutrient-density and vitamin richness of vegetables and fruits in general. Aim for a variety of different colored fruits and vegetables. However, if you don't have access to this, opt for green vegetables first. Vegetables like kale are considered *superfoods*. Calcium and iron are also great ways to alte

the mind positively.

Never give up on your dreams

The number one regret among men and women surveyed in their elder years is that they gave up on their dreams. Many times, even people who are successful in terms of money will report feeling sad about never having chased their dreams.

People simply seem to accept that dreaming big isn't practical, and thus not worthy of pursuit. While it's true that everyday life can get in the way, and that bills and debts aren't going to remove themselves, *never* give up on your dream. Find time in every day for your passion. If you're young especially, use your vitality to chase your dreams.

A lot of people have it backwards. As youngsters, they worry more about getting into some career so that they can start making money. They take less idealistic risks and are concerned more with building a foundation. Although this may make practical sense to some, it doesn't necessarily lead to happiness. Instead of worrying about money first and then thinking once you're settled you can chase your dreams, worry more about your dreams when you're capable—when you're young and able!

Too often the people who say they'll chase their dreams when they're older and settled are the same people who end up losing track of time. They look back and realize that the 9-5 became their defining path.

They never made the effort to go after what truly inspired them.

Defeating Depression & Anxiety—What You NEED to Know

Depression is a mystery.

The kind of dark, dangerous illness that creeps up on even the most stoic of humans. It doesn't matter if everything in your life is perfect or falling apart, depression can take its hold. At times, even those who seem the happiest, will fall to its clutches. Those who show the brightest smiles may bear the darkest voids.

We are often surprised by victims of depression. "But he has everything," we exclaim. "How could she be so sad?" we ask. "What went wrong and how?" Many times, we can't even admit that it exists. "There is no such thing as depression," we tell ourselves. "Being sad is just an excuse; a weakness. Life isn't meant to be easy." We shake our heads. "Depression is not a *real* illness."

But then it hits homes. Somebody close to us is falling apart. We hear of a suicide, or an attempt, a final, inexplicable act of defeat. We close our eyes and shake our heads when the news rings true.

"Robin Williams killed himself?"

And in the end, an illness, or disease we try to deny, is the same illness or disease that crushes our hearts. The truth of the matter is simple:

Depression is real. It's as real as any major mental disorder. As *real* as high blood pressure, diabetes, cancer and heart disease. Depression is a disease literally rooted in our brains, stretching to our bodies and bones. It is as much a product of our thoughts and feelings as it is chemical property of our brains; an *imbalance* in our brains.

But this is readily changed. Research shows that only 10% of happiness is affected b circumstances. In other words, it matters very little if you've experienced a terrible life or an objectively privileged one. What matters is your approach—your personality and your perception. Again, people with supposedly everything can feel like they have nothing. This can cause a variety of problems that then cause a world of hurt.

Before seeking a psychiatrist or meds, consider an <u>outlook overhaul</u>.

This includes:

1)   **Taking a deeper interest in others**. By focusing on how you can aid family and friends, you will be less focused on your own stressors. Of course, balance is key. Don't take on everybody else's problems as your own and become overburdened. After all, depression often stems from anxiety. When we constantly internalize our stress, we end up feeling hopeless. And this hopelessness, this helplessness, is a very real

precursor to depression.

So invest in others, but don't obsess over others. See how your actions better their lives, and focus less on what you can't or haven't changed.

2) **Being optimistic**. This is simplistic and commonsense, but worth repeating. The important thing to remember is that you can't control everything. So remove your ego from the equation. You're a person that matters, but the world does not revolve around you. If you think positively, everything in your world will change.

This is not a bunch of motivational b.s. It's a neurochemical fact. See the good in things, and the good will happen.

3) **Living with purpose**—another important thing to remember. This means that you care about your own potential. You see a future, and you actively work to achieve it. Many times, people with depression see no reason to go on. They wake up every day convinced that things don't matter. They look at the futility of life; they point to the fact that anybody can die at any time, that nobody knows *absolutely* what comes next. They are convinced that nothing will make their lives significant.

Frequently, this belief in the meaningless of life will cause a dark, downward spiral. Depression sufferers will turn to alcohol and drugs to erase their thoughts; to numb away the pain—or perhaps to fill the void with *something*. They'll give up on goals, visions, and dreams because, well, "what's the point?"

Other times, people with depression won't know why. Their minds will be weary, their thoughts and hopes dreary and dying. Many of them won't even know they're depressed. They'll think they're just tired or worn down; anxious or in pain.

It won't be until others point out the days, months, and years wasted, that the depressed individual comes to reality. In order to make this reality a positive one, sufferers must work proactively. They should consider what excites them, what achievements they are most proud of, and what they would like others to think of them. They should consider how they can take small, incremental changes. They should not shoot for an immense goal and expect to achieve it instantly. They should realize that very few people in life are handed a successful future, and even for those who are—how do we know they're truly happy?

Depression sufferers need not compare themselves to others they deem happier or more successful. If they focus on what drives them, they will not care what others have done. They will realize that everybody has a different trajectory, and that no two people should expect to be the same. Instead of resenting or envying others, sufferers will learn to appreciate the diversity of life, and its many fickle lessons.

4)   **The Moment**—Although having a purpose is important, it's more important to remember one fact: productivity does not equal purpose. In fact, many depressed people also fall at the other end of the spectrum. Instead of being dreary and listless, sitting in a dark room alone, some depressed individuals are out and about, *constantly*. These are the type that is hardest to address. They seem to be the happiest, the bubbliest. Their day are filled with activities and endeavors. They are constantly surrounded by a swarm of people—friends, family, and newfound acquaintances. These are the individuals who seem to have everything in the world, the type that touch countless lives with their warm spirits and generous hearts.

But they have a secret.

When they return home, when they spend that mere second, or minute, or hour alone, their lives crumble. Without consistent company, isolation ensues. Their thoughts turn dark and their spirits dwindle. The person everybody sees on the outside—the endlessly loving and lovable human—comes apart.

This is why savoring the moment is so critical. We learn to appreciate the small things, to embrace the restorative power of mindfulness. We learn to open our hearts and souls to life's little treasures. And most importantly, to ourselves.

When savoring the moment, we don't need to be endlessly surrounded with others. We appreciate the time spent in our thoughts, as well as detached from them. We are able to coexist with even our most negative emotions, knowing that they will pass—and will not define us. We learn who we are and what we want. Instead of mixing our own identity with the identities of others, we'll learn life's most important skill: knowing ourselves.

And when we know ourselves, when we can look fearlessly inward, and take inventory, everything else comes together. Our purpose, our perception, our relation to the many people, places and things that populate this life—all of it comes together.

And if we can see a reason for being here, in this moment, in this world, we will never have to be depressed again. And we will never have to feel like life is too hard, or too long, or too much for us to bare.

If we can learn to see something in everything, we will never run low. On reasons to smile.

A Special Note:

Thank you for reading *"A Reason to Smile: Finding Happiness in Life's Little Moments."*

And may you continue to live healthily and happily.

Sincerely,

C.K. Murray

Other works by C.K. Murray:

1. *Mindfulness Explained: The Mindful Solution to Stress, Depression, and Chronic Unhappiness*

2. *Emotional Intelligence Explained: How to Master Emotional Intelligence and Unlock Your True Ability*

3. *The Confidence Cure: Your Definitive Guide to Overcoming Low Self-Esteem, Learning Self-Love and Living Happily*

found my light amid the dark

Printed in Great Britain
by Amazon

62587870R20030